The
FINE ART
of
BEING VERTICAL

Surviving the Loss of a Child

The FINE ART of BEING VERTICAL

Surviving the Loss of a Child

Elizabeth Campbell Huntsman

Black Lyon Publishing, LLC

THE FINE ART OF BEING VERTICAL:
SURVIVING THE LOSS OF A CHILD
Copyright © 2013 by ELIZABETH CAMPBELL HUNTSMAN

All rights reserved.
No part of this book may be used or reproduced in any way by any means without the written permission of the publisher, except in the case of brief quotations embodied in critical articles and reviews.

Please note that if you have purchased this book without a cover or in any way marked as an advance reading copy, you have purchased a stolen item, and neither the author nor the publisher has been compensated for their work.

Our books may be ordered through your local bookstore or by visiting the publisher:

BlackLyonPublishing.com

Black Lyon Publishing, LLC
PO Box 567
Baker City, OR 97814

ISBN-10: 1-934912-55-7
ISBN-13: 978-1-934912-55-3

Written, published and printed in
the United States of America.

Black Lyon
NONFICTION

For Rick
Much loved and always remembered

Contents

Introduction	
How many Children do you have?	2
Sometimes People Say Helpful Things that Hurt	4
What do I do with my Child's Things?	6
Keeping Mementos	8
The Difference in the Manner of Loss	10
Guilt	12
Major Life Changes	14
Dealing with Holidays and Special Days	16
Faith and Grief	18
When Your Friends and Family Leave	20
A New Family Dynamic	22
Grief is Exhausting	24
Stuck in your Grief	26
Timetables	28
Age of the Child	30
Premonitions	32
Grieving Siblings	34
Living with Novocaine	36
Value Changes	38
Finding out Why	40
My Spouse Grieves Differently	42
Divorce, an Unexpected Consequence	44
How to Move On	46
Recognizing Acceptance	48
Service	50
Finding Beauty Again	52

Introduction

Losing a child is heart wrenching and obviously, life-altering. Some days it takes all your mental capacity just to remain standing. I know this firsthand, having lost a son almost fifteen years ago. I thought losing my mother at a young age was the worst possible grief I could know. In 1999, I learned I was wrong. I, along with David, my husband of more than forty years, still grieve for our son, Rick, who died in a car crash at the age of seventeen.

I've written THE FINE ART OF BEING VERTICAL as a workbook intended to be written in, to be cried over—and to help the grieving parent.

The name of the workbook is taken from the question often asked of those who grieve: "How are you?" Some days the answer can only be: "Vertical." And those are the good days.

Everyone travels the journey through grief at his or her own pace and with whatever support can be found. Yes, you can make it through this largest of life's challenges and no, it will not be easy. You loved your child deeply, so you must expect to grieve deeply.

There are several topics addressed in this workbook. Some will apply one day and others, another day. When someone becomes a grieving parent, he or she needs to know there is help. I hope this workbook will serve you when you don't yet feel able to seek out other help.

—Elizabeth Campbell Huntsman

How many Children do you have?

There is not an obstetrician alive who would consider that a woman has no children simply because her child is not living.

This is a fact: Once you are a parent, you are always a parent. It doesn't matter in the slightest how long you were able to love your child physically.

Many people who have lost a child flinch when asked this question and feel the need to explain. If that's what you feel you must do, then do it. The simplest thing to do is merely to answer, "Two." (Or whatever number of children you have.) Clearly and succinctly, include the child you can no longer hug with those you can.

Some people worry this makes people uncomfortable. You are a battle-scarred warrior in life, having taken the greatest blow there is and survived, so don't worry if people are uncomfortable. They'll get over it in a couple minutes and your child will live on.

Every now and again, you'll come across someone who will truly ask about your children and you'll feel comfortable sharing. They'll take your treasured memories in and you'll know that you've gained a friend of the heart.

WORKSHEET EXERCISES

Practice saying, "I have _____ children."

Practice stopping after you've said that.

Write a note to yourself. "I am the mother/father of _____ children.

Their names are:_____."

Practice saying your child is dead in a way you feel the listener would be comfortable with. Some might be:

Most listeners do not like to hear the words "death, dead, died." I can substitute: _____.

Practice saying that.

List what makes each of my children, living or not, special:

List why I am happy to have been a parent to each child:

Sometimes People Say "Helpful" Things that Hurt

In the first flush of grief most people agree that the primary emotion is shock. When we are in shock we are seldom able to function efficiently. This is particularly true when people wish to offer condolences in the loss of a child. We have all been recipients of these condolences and a few of us have received odd or hurtful words from those who should care about us.

There are a couple of reasons for this. The first is that the condoler simply didn't think about what he was saying, awash as he was in his own grief. If a person, for example, says, "It's lucky you have other children," the parent may take that as devaluing the lost one. If this situation applies to us, such words simply don't help. Children are not interchangeable and the fact that we are lucky to have others doesn't mitigate our loss.

Secondly, every now and again, a grief-stricken parent will find that a "friend" is not true. This was the case when a parent was told, "You need to find out what you're doing wrong and stop it so God will stop punishing you." This is not a good friend and, while it's unfortunate that such words come during high emotions, a grieving parent needs distance from family or friends like this.

Finally, a saddened parent's senses are often on hyper-alert. Sometimes we don't perceive the thought behind the words. It does us no good to dwell on what might have been meant.

WORKSHEET EXERCISES

When _____ told me _____,

I felt _____.

It helped a lot when _____ said:

It helped a lot when _____ said:

_____ told me:

I think what was really meant was:

I don't know if I can forgive _____ for saying:

I resolve that, when and if this happens again, I'll say:
1.
2.
3.

What Do I Do with my Child's Things?

This seems to be an area where many people are willing to offer advice to bereft parents. And, it also seems a topic where most people have opinions.

First of all, do not let anyone talk you into doing something you don't want to do, if it does not **absolutely** have to be done.

Next, consider if you can, what you really need to remain the same. Your world has been turned upside-down in your loss and it can never be the same. Think about what will give you comfort.

Some parents leave a child's room as it was. This is fine for awhile. "Awhile" lends itself to many interpretations. Generally, most parents feel they can address this at or before the one-year mark.

Other parents clean up every evidence of the child from the home, leaving only pictures in an album. This is not common, but if it's right for you and you are not destructive, it's fine.

It is often easier if manageable goals are set so that this doesn't loom as a huge task. It is also helpful if a parent can do this with a trusted friend. Choose your support person carefully as this can be a brutal chore and you will need sensitivity.

Finally, many people find it comforting to put the important things from a child's life into boxes. Many parents never look through them again but find this a comforting connection.

You should do what's right for *you*. If you find yourself, five years down the road, maintaining a shrine to your dead child, it's time to seek professional help.

WORKSHEET EXERCISES

I will change the sheets on my child's bed by: _____

These things are very close to my heart and I want them nearby:
1.
2.
3.

I can box up the following:
1.
2.
3.

_____would be a person I can ask to help me.

A good use for my child's room would be:

A safe place to keep the boxes would be:

Keeping Mementos

One of the ways we grieve is to try and keep as much as we can the same. As is written elsewhere in this workbook, we need to know what to do with our child's things.

When we have decided what (if anything) to do, it will be difficult to do it.

Oftentimes parents will have mementos to remember all their children. These can be things that celebrate a child's life, something they used or loved, or merely something that reminds us of them.

It is common for parents of means to do things like endow scholarships or name building for their children. For many parents these sorts of things are not options. But, we each can do things on a smaller scale, such as sending a child to camp or planting a tree.

Sometimes service is the memento. While often intangible, volunteerism can help us remember our child. Mothers Against Drunk Driving (MADD) was founded by a mother who lost her child to a drunk driver. Cancer has walks and runs and the Suicide Prevention Program can use both money and volunteers.

Many parents find writing to be an excellent way to remember their child. While it will memorialize your child, it is also very therapeutic for you.

WORKSHEET EXERCISES

What mementos will provide a good picture of my child?

Who will benefit?

How much money can I spend?

Will doing this bring my child to more than just me?

Do I need to have people get to know my child?

A list of less-costly mementos:
1.
2.
3.

A "dream" list, if money is no object:
1.
2.
3.

How does what I've chosen celebrate my child's existence?

The Difference in the Manner of the Loss

Parents whose children die suddenly and unexpectedly often grieve differently from those whose children die from chronic and terminal illnesses.

Both parents go through the so-called "steps" of grief, beginning with denial. One difference is, the latter parents may go through some of the steps (like denial) while their child lives.

Occasionally, these same parents progress far enough in their grieving that they are relieved when their child is no longer suffering. However, parents in both situations grieve the loss, the actual "missing" of the child, exactly the same.

A parent's world is turned upside-down in a sudden death. In a chronic illness, it had been tilting for some time.

The actual grieving process is the same in both instances because the child is simply—gone.

WORKSHEET EXERCISES

The biggest shock in the death of my child happened when:

What I would say to a parent whose child died in a manner similar to mine:

What I would say if it were different:

Was I in denial?

When did it set in?

How long did it last?

Do I have flashes of denial now?

Can I make it to Acceptance?

Will I need support?

What kind?

Where will I go for it?

Guilt

Many bereaved parents feel guilt in one degree or another. This is reasonable because we parents are charged with the protection of our children. When they die we might feel as if we had failed in our duty to protect them. This guilt is real and, to a degree, reasonable. There are many kinds of guilt.

If a child died due to an illness, a parent may feel guilt for having passed along "bad genes." This is something over which few people have control.

Perhaps your child died as a direct result of your actions, such as in a hunting or motor vehicle accident. The key here is to realize these are *accidents*. Brutal, ugly accidents.

Another time parents feel guilty is when a child is lost to suicide. No parent expects a child to commit suicide, but a child may exercise his free will and do this. We can remember that hindsight is always more clear than foresight.

To that end, parents sometimes feel as if they should have foreseen and recognized indicators such as poor driving skills, poor choices of friends, and substance abuse.

A child who dies in service to his or her country may cause us to feel guilty when all around people are celebrating the child's bravery and valor. It may take years before we recognize what was bought at the price of our child's life. Guilt is a real feeling, whether or not it is justified.

WORKSHEET EXERCISES

Do I feel guilty?

Why or why not?

Things I did wrong as a parent:
1.
2.

How I would do them right if I had another chance:
1.
2.

Things I did right as a parent:
1.
2.
3.
4.

Ways guilt can rule my life:
1.
2.
3.

Am I willing to let guilt take over my life and focus?

If I continue to feel deeply guilty and know that it is deserved, who can I talk to?

Who can refer me to a counselor?

Major Life Changes

It is ridiculous to assume parents could face anything they might consider a "major life change" when the most major of all life changes has already occurred in the loss of their child.

Nevertheless, most "advisors" will say that a grieving person should plan no other major life changes in the first year following the death of the child.

This is sound advice, but does not always apply in every instance.

Sometimes a process of change may be underway at the time of loss. Other times the loss may necessitate the change.

In any case, people saddled with grief should think long and hard about all the changes they make and why they make them.

For example, a person in the throes of grief might feel unable to look at a child's empty bedroom. Selling a home is very hard to undo when the parent discovers that he or she misses the supportive neighbor. Mementos should not be disposed of and lifestyle changes such as a new religion/minister should be very cautiously attempted.

Since it is difficult to judge and reason while mired in sorrow, it is good advice to postpone as many major life changes as possible for the first year following the death of your child.

WORKSHEET EXERCISES

Something I would like to change:

The benefits of that would be:
1.
2.
3.

The drawbacks would be:
1.
2.
3.

Why do I want change?

What will happen if I don't make the change?

If I do?

Does my family support this change?

Can this change wait a year?

Why or why not?

Dealing with Holidays and Special Days

A word often used in dealing with grief is "brutal." There is no way to sugar coat it, and we wouldn't, but that's the right word in describing a grieving parent's emotions on special days.

So much of the joy of holidays is wrapped in each family's traditions. Examples are, for Christmas: time to open presents, family gatherings, ornaments, games, etc.

There is no way that the first holidays will be easy. It's not even probable they will be bearable. Knowing that, there are a few things one can do to help them pass without too much added agony.

We have traditions because we love them. They make us feel safe and comfortable. After a child dies, we re-examine our traditions. For holidays, people fall into three camps: those who tweak traditions because of loss, those who try to keep everything the same, and those who completely change what has gone before.

Only you will know what's right for you and your family. Some families have gone on cruises for Christmas and felt that they did the absolute right thing. Others want things to remain, as much as possible, as they were. Those families who choose to change some of their traditions do so because they believe it will help them make it through the holidays.

Do not be surprised if you feel the need for extra support during holidays. Birthdays, weddings and graduations also can be especially tough, so be aware.

WORKSHEET EXERCISES

Our holiday traditions are:
1.
2.
3.

It is important that I keep the following tradition:

A tradition I can omit or change is:

When the grief hits especially hard, I can call:

A way to make my child part of the holiday would be:

It is important that I be able to talk about my child amidst all the celebration. Those who will encourage this are:

When I weep a safe place to do that is:

No one is allowed to tell me not to cry.

Now and then, I will try to look beyond my grief. If I can't, that's okay, too.

Faith and Grief

Each of us has some sort of belief system. Many believe generally in a Higher Power and others have very specific beliefs. Some believe we are entirely responsible for ourselves and that this life is all there is. A few don't really know what they believe, only what they don't believe.

Examine your beliefs and hold to that which you know beyond any doubt. Comfort will come, little by little, when you cling to what you know.

If you believe we exist after this life, take comfort in that. If you want to believe that, search for it. If you believe there is only this life, do something to make it count.

No one who is a true friend should tell you what you should believe spiritually.

In our journey through life we refine what we believe. The death of a child forces us to consider our belief system, clinging to what we hold dear.

Any support system that helps a person progress is a good one.

WORKSHEET EXERCISES

I believe the following without a doubt:
1.
2.
3.

I think the following:
1.
2.
3.

I wonder about:
1.
2.
3.

People who believe the same as I do are:

If I need a spiritual answer, I can go to:

What do I need to do to put my belief system into action?

Do I believe this is a test of my faith?

Does my belief system make me feel better?   How?

When your Friends and Family Leave

When a loss strikes us, the natural tendency of those who love us is to comfort us. Mostly they do this by being with us and loving us.

Few of us, however, have a support system that can continue indefinitely. Our support system people will have to go back to their own lives, jobs and families. It is a scary thing to face grief by ourselves.

When we are cosseted by family members or friends, there are very few decisions we must make. Food is provided, housework done, work avoided.

Eventually people must leave us. While they still care deeply for us and share our grief, they will have to leave. This is usually very frightening.

Sometimes it is helpful to work up to being alone by making some minor decisions. Even if you don't feel it, reassure people you will be able to handle this. You must try, and if you simply cannot, find a support group or counselor and be dedicated in going.

Life, in reality, does not stop just because your world ended.

WORKSHEET EXERCISES

To prepare for being on your own, choose what you'll have for breakfast. How much were you able to eat?

Choose a room to tidy up and do it. If you sob during the vacuuming, let yourself.

Will you be able to return to your workplace?   Must you?

What changes are necessary so that you can be functional on your own?

Can you make those changes?

How will you let your family and friends help even when they are not in your immediate vicinity?

List ways that you can know that you are loved:

A New Family Dynamic

When parents start a family, their children come in a semblance of order. If an older child dies, the younger children have lost a leader. If a younger one dies, the older one may feel guilt or responsibility.

So, how does the dynamic in a family change?

A family with one child who loses him or her does not become childless. They are still parents. Many people who have not experienced this deepest of all grief do not understand this.

A child who loses an older sibling does not become the oldest child. He may function in some ways as such, but he knows he is not. The same idea is true for the loss of a younger child.

Your family will, assuredly, have a hole in it. It can still be functional, even strong, but you must recognize the hole. It cannot be filled, but it demands recognition.

If a family has three children and one dies, does the parent then say he has two children? No, if a child dies it does not mean he or she has ceased to exist. But, people are not always anxious to hear an explanation of why you say you have three children.

In the family dynamic, a grieving parent is still a parent.

WORKSHEET EXERCISES

My child, _____, made an impact on our family in the following way:

_____ was #_____ in order.

Special characteristics _____ had because of this were:
1.
2.
3.

When people ask after my children, I will say:

I recognize the makeup of my family has changed. Some differences are:
1.
2.
3.

Some things that remain the same are:
1.
2.
3.

How can I strengthen my family?

Grief is Exhausting

Grieving will wear you out, yet many people find it difficult to rest, relax or sleep.

There are reasons we cannot sleep—the first being fear of surrendering to dreams. This fear is probably mostly about control. After the loss of a child there's not much in life under our control. Also, all of our senses are on "hyper-alert" to protect whatever loved ones we retain.

Another reason some have difficulty sleeping is that, after some time in not sleeping, we may have forgotten how.

But, our health will surely suffer if we do not rest.

Short-term medication may help re-train our bodies to sleep. However, our sleep patterns may be forever altered. We'll need to find out what our new "normal" is. A good plan is to force yourself into a routine, but be gentle.

If, several months after the loss, you find you cannot relax enough to sleep, it may be time to share your grief with a trusted friend, a clergyman, your physician or a mental health counselor. Any time counseling is recommended (and there is no shame in seeking this sort of help) be aware it may take a while to find a counselor who fits.

WORKSHEET EXERCISES

I slept adequately on: _____.

I will pick a specific bedtime and prepare myself to be in bed at that time.

Things I'll share with a counselor if and when I pick one:
1.
2.
3.

What I will do so I can rest:

"Tricks" I've learned to help me relax:

I dreamed of my child, _____.

A good dream was:

Stuck in your Grief

Now and then a person becomes mired in grief. Those who are familiar with emotional mud bogs know they are, to put it mildly, unpleasant.

A person mired in grief cannot function. Just as with the mud, a parent can be stuck.

Each of us spends time, as we grieve, in a mire. Sometimes with a lot of effort on our part, we pull ourselves out. Other times, kind people pull us out.

How do we recognize when we are at a standstill and stuck?

Our heart will tell us when we are no longer progressing. Negative thoughts will overpower us and deep depression will set in. We may have to rely on others to point this out, but we should be receptive.

What can we do?

We should try every day for progress, even if it is tiny little steps. We must realize we may need help. We can take ownership of our personal quagmire and become the boss of it.

We can emerge from the mud, tired and dirty. Tired and dirty, but able to move forward.

WORKSHEET EXERCISES

My most difficult quagmire is:

Warning signs for me that I'm not progressing:
1.
2.
3.

I made progress from the mire by doing:

Who can I trust to tell me how I'm doing?

Who is someone who will tell me?

Do I value that opinion?

What kinds of dirt and grime do I bring from a bog?

Do I believe there is a timetable for the grieving process?

Why or why not?

Timetables

Many people, both those watching and those experiencing it, expect there to be a timetable for grief.

This is unrealistic. Since each parent is an individual, each parent will process the loss differently. And, each watcher will have different concepts of what grief should be.

Do not be bound by timetables. Try instead to make a little progress each day. For example, recognize the day when you don't cry in the car. Recognize when you are able to go in that child's room. Try and say your child's name out loud, then try to talk with someone about your child.

People often refer to the first year as "brutal" and it is. Every day is a "first"—the first Halloween without your child, the first football season, the first birthday …

While it is perfectly normal to want to sit tight for that first year, please know there is nothing magical about it. On the 370th day after you've buried your child, you will still miss him or her. Sometimes, years after, you will be hit with tears—sometimes they will be little ones that you can brush away with the back of a hand and sometimes not.

Rather than thinking of a timetable for grief, consider that progress means you are moving forward, and try for that.

WORKSHEET EXERCISES

Things I need to do:
1.
2.
3.

What is stopping me?

When was I able to speak on the telephone, cry, but continue the conversation?

My plan for progressing through grief is:

My plan for adjusting that plan:

Who tells me I'm not adhering to a grief timeline?

Who comforts me and recognizes that tiny steps forward are progress?

What happens when I don't make progress?

What should I do?

Age of the Child

Each loss is unique, even to parents who have lost more than one child.

A parent who loses a child at or before birth naturally grieves for what might have been and what will be missed. The parent grieves for not knowing the child, and they wonder.

When a child dies in the middle years, while he or she is still at home, parents grieve for the spark of potential they saw extinguished. They grieve the loss of the individual they knew and loved.

Sometimes a child is an adult, perhaps with children of his or her own. This brings, not surprisingly, yet a different grief. Then, a parent also grieves with those who share this loss.

We may have difficulty understanding why some people grieve in ways we wouldn't if we happened to be in their shoes.

Recognizing the many differences and yet appreciating a common denominator is not always easy. We do not know how we'll respond to this heartbreaking grief until we are faced with it.

A child is a child, and he or she is very lucky to have been loved enough by a family that they sorrow at his/her death. The age of a child presents different grief parameters to the parents, but each passing does come with grief and we cannot judge another's response.

WORKSHEET EXERCISES

My child, _____, was _____ years, _____ months, _____ days old at death.

I think I would've liked to have known my child in 20 years. I think I would see:

I'm writing the following letter to my child:

Premonitions

Many bereaved parents feel that if they had paid attention, there were portents, omens and premonitions that could have prevented this situation. That may be. Or not.

We cannot change anything as final as death, and it's never productive to play the "what if" game.

Guilt often figures in when people remember premonitions. It also happens that, when the most dreaded of all occurs, our senses are heightened. We remember clearly things that may have been hazy when they happened. We interpret portents to fit what happened. Omens become clear.

If we assume that these premonitions and the like are seated in our brains, it is reasonable to assume also that we can communicate in other ways besides verbally and with body language.

When we consider premonitions after the loss of a child, we are always considering them after the fact. Premonitions do happen, especially regarding our children.

WORKSHEET EXERCISES

A premonition about my child that I had was:

Do I remember how it felt when I had this premonition?

What did I change because of it?

What did I not change?

Why did I make (or not) changes?

Other, unrelated, premonitions I have had were:
1.
2.
3.

How did I respond to them?

Why do I have premonitions?

Grieving Siblings

Probably the single most-mentioned worry a grieving parent has: My child's siblings grieve and I'm too lost in my own sorrow to help.

The death of a child often takes every ounce of our power to exist. We simply cannot focus on anyone else's needs because our own are not being met.

The loss of a sibling is intense, yet very different from what a parent feels.

When you are unable to help your own children, there are a few options.

It is often helpful to keep a diary. There are books to help. And there are people who can help.

The last may prove the most beneficial.

A good counselor may help your child on his journey. Caring friends and relatives may help. Fellow members of your church or belief system may be willing to help.

Whatever you choose to do, please address this challenge and do something. The fact you've lost one child does not make the surviving ones less precious; it merely means your focus has necessarily shifted.

WORKSHEET EXERCISES

I am concerned about my child's siblings because:

My child's siblings express their grief by:
1.
2.
3.
4.

Is this positive?

Someone who could help my surviving children is:

A letter to my living children:

Living With Novocaine

Many times the agony a bereft parent feels manifests itself physically and can be debilitating.

Those who have been to a dentist and have had that dentist drilling away and hitting a nerve know intense pain. It is usually easily managed with Novocaine—sometimes a truckload of it.

Our grief is an exposed nerve that usually gets in the way of living our lives. Different people with different needs use different kinds of Novocaine.

The most destructive Novocaine of all is that which is obsessively self-prescribed. Alcohol and over-the-counter drugs can be misused. This abuse of drugs often begins as self-medication.

If you feel you need something beyond what is gentle and easily available, be prepared for a visit, to begin with, to your primary care provider. The provider should know you and can assess your needs. You will either be given a prescription and specific instructions, or you will be given a referral.

If you need pharmaceutical help, do not be ashamed. It is much like a person with a broken leg who needs a crutch. As a parent, your diagnosis is that you have a broken heart. Novocaine, in whatever form, gives you time and energy to heal.

When you no longer need the crutch, you should toss it.

WORKSHEET EXERCISES

I believe people who use drugs as a crutch are:

I believe that medicine *should* or *should not* be used as a crutch. (Circle one)

I most need medical intervention when:

How do I feel about "taking something" to help?

Who do I trust to know my needs and help me have what I need?

What do I do to "self-medicate"?

Is this healthy?

What do I expect drugs to do for me?

For how long?

Value Changes

In our society each of us has the opportunity to make a myriad of choices. We can decide how we wish to earn a living, where we want to live, how (or if) we want to worship, and many more. Extremely challenging situations, such as the death of a child, often force us to evaluate these choices.

While we cannot go back and change our values, we can go forward and do so. Many people feel change is necessary.

We may change the amount of time/effort we spend on our livelihood. If we have surviving children at home, we may spend less time. If we do not, we may spend more time. Or, we may use it as an escape.

We may change where and how we live. While not making any major changes for a year, we may choose to live differently.

We may choose to change how (or if) we worship. Nothing forces a spiritual evaluation like the loss of a child.

We may wonder what to do with the inheritance we had earmarked for the dead child. There are a lot of options. Many people want a legacy for the child while others divide among the surviving children.

We may change how we behave toward family members. Some people renew fractured relationships and others move away, feeling they're not worth the effort.

WORKSHEET EXERCISES

The most important personal value I have is:

Others are:
1.
2.
3.

What will happen if I change the value,_____ _____?

Can I deal with that?

How do I feel about extended family?

Do I want to renew relationships?   Is it worth the effort?

What do I want to do about my child's inheritance?

Is this about me or about a legacy for my child?

What do I have to do to make sure my wishes are followed?

Do I wish to examine my spiritual beliefs?

Do I know what they are?

If I do, how do I go about it?

What values will define my life?

Finding out Why

Distraught parents occasionally become obsessed with "why." There are a lot of whys.

Why did this happen? It makes no sense.

Why did the same thing happen to someone else and their child is alive?

Why don't we get a second chance?

Why, why, why.

If we dwell on these whys, they will become an ocean that will engulf us. We need to differentiate between what matters and will matter to others *and* what we need to accept.

We hear stories of parents who made their child's death a crusade. As previously mentioned, MADD was founded by one such woman.

Most of us will not become crusaders. Most of us may make changes, such as making sure a seat belt is fastened or a driver is sober. We may walk for the cancer cure. We may plant a tree.

The whys exist in some measure to validate our child's life. When we realize our child's life is validated because we, as parents, loved him or her best of all, many of the whys will fade.

WORKSHEET EXERCISES

The biggest "why" I have is:

Another why I don't understand is:

The differences between someone else and my child are:

Does this make a difference?

What can I do to validate my child's life?
1.
2.
3.

Changes I can make in my life:
1.
2.
3.

Whys that are not worth pursuing:
1.
2.
3.

Whys that are:

My Spouse Grieves Differently

Two individuals are faced with a horrendous situation. Of course they will each respond individually.

Oftentimes we become caught up so much in our grief we fail to see the hurt others suffer. We believe our way to grieve is the only way and that anyone who doesn't cry as much or as often as we do is not as sad.

Or, we simply can't understand why someone we love can't get over it and move on. Like we have.

As we all know only too well, there are as many different faces to grief as there are to those who sorrow.

Grieving together can be a time that draws spouse and/or family closer together. On occasion though, grief can be a wedge that drives people who love each other apart.

Do not judge the depth of another's grief by your own. If possible, talk about the differences. Remember you each came to the relationship with a history that makes your responses different. Neither has to be right or wrong.

Men and women often deal differently with grief. Women generally find it easier to reach out for support while men believe they can "handle it." Both are acceptable responses.

WORKSHEET EXERCISES

I wish my spouse understood:

I don't understand when my spouse does:

Things I would like to talk about together
1.
2.
3.

Do I think my spouse loves our child more or less than I do?

I wish I could handle this like:

Because:

What I admire about my spouse:

Divorce, an Unexpected Consequence

Many of us travel through life without ever fully understanding our own relationships. A divorce or separation can occur when one party wants it, no matter what the other wants. Sometimes in a marriage two people simply grow apart and the death of a child is merely the catalyst for the dissolution of a long-dead marriage. Regardless of why, a divorce on the heels of a child's death is not uncommon.

If we consider that a child's death is the worst loss, then we must realize the strain that puts on any relationship. Sometimes in grief, people grow together and other times, apart. It seldom happens that anything is ever the same again.

So, what does one do to keep a marriage or other relationship intact? The single most important thing is to include the other in your grieving. Do not shut him or her out.

It is always a good idea to have some good joint counseling. Sometimes having another person in the room makes it possible to discuss issues openly. Many friends can recommend good counselors.

Recognize if one party is truly intent on ending a marriage, acceptance may be the only avenue open to you.

WORKSHEET EXERCISES

The strongest aspects of my marriage are:

Where we need to work:

On a scale of one to ten, where do I rank my marriage vows?

Where does my partner?

A counselor who might be helpful is:

Things I would like my partner to know that would hurt too much if I said them out loud:

How has this child's death affected our relationship?

How to Move On

This topic is extremely touchy for most grieving parents.

The problem is, others want us to "move on" when we may not feel ready to do so. When someone tells us we need to do this, a knee-jerk response might be, "&%*#@$%!" However, this is **not** productive and often makes the grieving parent feel guilty.

So, to reiterate what has been said many times over, move at your own speed.

Everyone has crutches. Often it's the boxes of belongings, safely stored but seldom looked at. Sometimes it's a wall ornament or other memento. Now and again, it's your child's friends.

If you sit with your personal crutch every night and cry over it, if you make the memento into a shrine, or if you try and run the surviving friends' lives, then you may not be progressing.

Whether or not you move on is up to you. You may certainly stay where you are, especially if it's safe. You may know there's more you want from life or you may know others need or depend on you. If the latter is the case, you may elect to try and move ahead.

Moving on does not mean you have forgotten your child. It just means the grief of his or her passing is no longer your main focus. This is good. But, difficult.

WORKSHEET EXERCISES

How do I feel when people say I need to move on?

Is there some validity to them saying that?

Why am I afraid to move ahead?

These scary things may happen if I move on.
1.
2.
3.

What will I do if I am able to move on?
1.
2.
3.

Are these things I want to do?

What are the goals I have for the balance of my life?

Can I achieve them from where I am now?

Recognizing Acceptance
(You can't change it.)

Many saddened parents find it odd to realize it is possible to go through life with a great, gaping hole in the heart. There will come a point when that huge hole in your heart is not the focus of everything you do in life.

No matter how you wish life had dealt differently with you, you will recognize that what happened, happened.

Sometimes this knowledge comes little bit by little bit, and sometimes it happens like a lightning bolt.

Eventually, it will happen.

Can we hurry the acceptance phase along? The nature of grief is that it takes over our lives and becomes our master. Our job is to replace grief with acceptance and move on, holey heart and all.

You will know you are approaching acceptance when you hear a bird sing. When you smile. When you help someone. When you can sing a silly song. When you can delight in someone else's child, one who is alive and well.

One day, you will realize your heart has a scar and the hole is shrinking. You will realize you are healing.

WORKSHEET EXERCISES

Things I know for sure:
1.
2.
3.

Things I wish I didn't know, but nevertheless know are true:
1.
2.
3.

People I can help include:
1.
2.
3.

The hole in my heart is what percentage of my heart?

What did the hole in my heart knock out?

How can I get the lost parts of my heart back?

Does accepting mean forgetting?   Why or why not?

Service

As we move along the journey that is grief, we will make it to a point where we want to help others.

There are many levels of help, from prayer to holding a sobbing parent. No one expects a saddened parent to put grief behind and immediately move out into the world helping others. Like a ladder, we need to begin at the bottom rung.

Almost any bereft parent welcomes any prayer. It shouldn't matter what the belief is, a prayer from the heart is good for everyone.

Up the ladder a bit is the "almost" connection. These are those things such as sympathy cards. No direct contact is essential. A telephone call is very difficult and several more rungs up the ladder.

One of the most challenging methods of service is the personal visit or attending a child's funeral. Be prepared for people to exclaim, "Oh, you know how I feel!" It may seem obvious, but only you know how *you* feel. You know that in a similar situation your personal grief was almost overpowering.

Why do service, if it's such a challenge? It's because of the ladder. Every time we put someone else's feelings ahead of ours, we climb up a little bit out of the mire of grief.

You do *not* need to forget about your child to do service. Many grieving parents find solace in discussing their child with others who understand. Newly grief-stricken parents appreciate tremendously that someone comes who can listen and who has walked on their path.

Service takes many forms and only you know what you are ready to do. If you come to a person's house and find yourself unable to get out of your car and ring the doorbell, take comfort in the fact you tried. Then, go home and write them a letter. You will feel better.

WORKSHEET EXERCISES

A service I would like to do is:

I could go to another child's funeral in:
- A week
- Six months
- A year
- Five years
- Never

What sort of stamps should go on a condolence card?

What would I say to a parent in my position?

How can I show those I love that I love them?

Finding Beauty Again

Many grief-stricken parents think they will never again see any beauty in a world without their child.

When a gorgeous sunrise occurs a parent might feel it's just one more day without the child. Or, the parent may not even recognize the sun has come up.

If a parent has an opportunity to make something beautiful, such as a performance, craft or art, it often occurs that these efforts take a decidedly dark turn.

When there are options in how to perceive a situation, a grieving parent may choose the more negative.

Most parents recognize it's their perception that has changed. Daffodils may still bloom, but they are for others to appreciate.

Most bereft parents simply don't have the capacity for joy. It has to be relearned and reintegrated into their lives. While relearning to appreciate beauty can be difficult, parents are often surprised that one day they find themselves singing along with the radio.

The choice to look for silver linings does not happen overnight. When a parent finally sees some beauty he or she may, the next minute, regret that knowledge. Grief is a process.

WORKSHEET EXERCISES

The most beautiful thing I ever saw was:

Recently I was with someone who said that the following was beautiful, pretty, or lovely:

I will look for beauty in the following places:

I can make something beautiful and it will be:

A good thing that happened recently was:

I will be around positive people. Some are:
1.
2.
3.

Joy is a choice. I choose joy by:

Each of the seasons brings its unique beauty.

Spring:

Summer:

Fall:

Winter:

*"It was in the midst of winter that I finally
learned that there was in me an invincible summer."*
— Albert Camus

•

AMAZING GRACE

Lopez-Kowalkowski verses

And now I'm free from chains of woe;
I leaned on Thee, O Lord.
Thy endless love for me I know;
My weeping prayers Thou heard.

My broken heart is full of love;
I'll show my love to thee
By singing praise to God above
And know Eternity.

•

May you find your invincible summer and, along the way,
learn to take being vertical for granted.
—ECH

NOTES:

NOTES:

NOTES:

www.ingramcontent.com/pod-product-compliance
Lightning Source LLC
Chambersburg PA
CBHW081455060426
42444CB00037BA/3285